North American Animals
Coloring Book by Christine Karron

Recommended for coloring with colored pencils,
markers, pens and/or crayons.
If using wet media place a sheet of thick paper or card
behind the coloring page to prevent bleed through.

All illustrations in this coloring book were originally created and
completely hand drawn by the artist Christine Karron.
Please visit www.chkarron.com for more about Christine's artwork.

Swirl Spirit
North American Animals
Coloring book by Christine Karron
First published December 2016

ISBN-13: 978-1541210025
ISBN-10: 1541240022

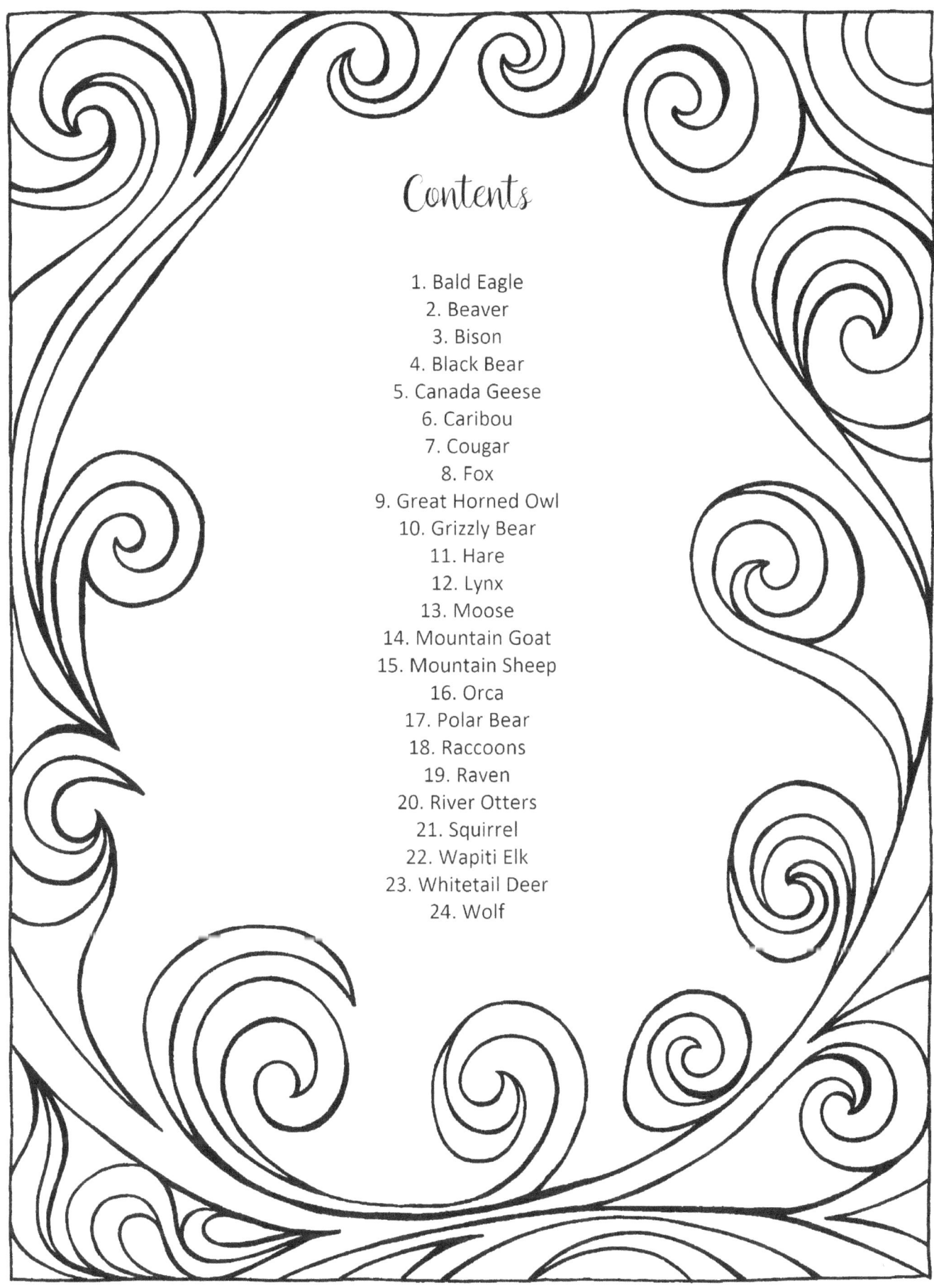

Contents

Bald Eagle

Swirl Spirits North American Animals Coloring Book by Christine Karron

Beaver

Black Bear

Canada Geese

Swirl Spirits North American Animals Coloring Book by Christine Karron

Caribou

Cougar

Fox

Great Horned Owl

Grizzly Bear

Hare

.

Swirl Spirits North American Animals Coloring Book by Christine Karron

Moose

Mountain Goat

Mountain Sheep

Orca

Raven

River Otters

Swirl Spirits North American Animals Coloring Book by Christine Karron

Squirrel

Whitetail Deer

Swirl Spirits North American Animals Coloring Book by Christine Karron

Wolf